THE STORY OF THE WRIGHT BROTHERS

A Biography Book for New Readers

Written by
Annette Whipple

Illustrated by
Alessandra Santelli

ROCKRIDGE
PRESS

D0958926

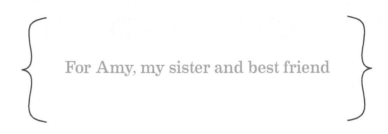

For Amy, my sister and best friend

For general information on our other products and services or to obtain technical support, please contact our Customer Care Department within the United States at (866) 744-2665, or outside the United States at (510) 253-0500.

Rockridge Press publishes its books in a variety of electronic and print formats. Some content that appears in print may not be available in electronic books, and vice versa.

TRADEMARKS: Rockridge Press and the Rockridge Press logo are trademarks or registered trademarks of Callisto Media Inc. and/or its affiliates, in the United States and other countries, and may not be used without written permission. All other trademarks are the property of their respective owners. Rockridge Press is not associated with any product or vendor mentioned in this book.

Series Designer: Angela Navarra
Interior and Cover Designer: Angela Navarra
Art Producer: Hannah Dickerson
Editor: Orli Zuravicky
Production Editor: Nora Milman

Illustrations © Alessandra Santelli, 2020. Maps courtesy of Creative Market. Photographs: Alamy Stock Photo/World History Archive, p. 50; Alamy Stock Photo/The History Collection, p. 51; Alamy Stock Photo/Hilary Morgan, p. 52. Author photo courtesy of Dorie Duquette

ISBN: Print 978-1-64739-239-0 | eBook 978-1-64739-240-6

R1

CONTENTS

CHAPTER 1

TWO HIGHFLIERS ARE BORN

Meet Wilbur and Orville Wright

Impossible! Most people thought a flying machine would never work. For hundreds of years, people had been trying to figure out how to fly. Even the brilliant **inventor** Leonardo da Vinci had ideas about flight all the way back in the 1400s! That was more than 400 years before Wilbur and Orville Wright did the "impossible." They were the first to build and fly an airplane in 1903.

How did the Wright brothers figure out how to fly when so many others couldn't? They didn't go to college. They weren't rich. But Wilbur and Orville had big imaginations, and they knew how to solve problems.

Wilbur and Orville were curious kids. They wanted to know more ... about everything. When they grew up, they were still curious, and they were still a team. It took years and years,

but they didn't give up. They learned the science of flying. They figured out how to build and control an airplane. They taught themselves how to fly. Finally, on December 17, 1903, Wilbur and Orville Wright did the impossible. They flew!

> **We were lucky** enough to grow up in an environment where there was always **much encouragement to children** to pursue intellectual interests.
>
> —ORVILLE WRIGHT

The Wright Brothers' America

JUMP –IN THE– THINK TANK

How would your life be different if you lived in the 1800s without phones, cars, or even electricity?

The brothers were born shortly after the **American Civil War** ended in 1865. This war was fought between the states in the North and the states in the South over states' rights, including **slavery**. After nearly four years, the war was over, and the country was one nation again. Unfortunately, Americans still disagreed about slavery and how to fix America.

In 1867, Wilbur Wright was born near Millville, Indiana. The family moved to Dayton, Ohio, where Orville Wright was born in 1871. Life was different then. When the Wright brothers were born, people traveled by horse and buggy. They had to—the car hadn't been invented yet! The

WHERE?

OHIO

MILLVILLE

INDIANA

DAYTON

fastest way to travel was by railroad. There were no light bulbs or telephones. Without indoor plumbing, most families (including the Wrights) still needed to leave their houses to use the bathroom. They used an outdoor hut called an outhouse.

4

There were no airplanes when the Wright brothers were boys, but there was a flying toy. It was a toy helicopter powered by rubber bands. Wilbur and Orville had one. They called it a "bat." The flying toy made the boys wonder about flight. They loved it! Orville even tried to build one when he should have been studying in school.

When the Wright brothers grew up, they would invent the first powered airplane that could carry a person. Their work changed the world. Who were these brothers? Just *how* did they make the first airplane?

American Civil War begins. **1861**

American Civil War ends. **1865**

Wilbur Wright is born. **1867**

North America's first cross-country railroad is finished. **1869**

Orville Wright is born. **1871**

CHAPTER 2
THE EARLY YEARS

Family Ties

Wilbur and Orville weren't just brothers, they were best friends. Their dad called them inseparable because they did everything together. The boys had a loving family. Reuchlin and Lorin were their big brothers. Next came Wilbur. Then Orville was born four years later. Their little sister, Katharine, arrived on Orville's third birthday.

The children wanted to know about their world. Their parents, Milton and Susan Wright, helped them learn. Mr. Wright filled their house with books. Mrs. Wright helped the kids understand how things worked. She showed them how to take things apart and put them back together. Sometimes Wilbur and Orville forgot to clean up after their projects. Their mom didn't mind. She just moved their projects to a kitchen shelf.

The family moved a lot. Mr. Wright was a pastor for the United Brethren Church in Christ. Some years he was also a **bishop** for the church, which meant he was in charge of churches in his area. Sometimes he had to move closer to new churches. The family moved from Indiana to Ohio and then to Iowa. Moving wasn't easy, but they had each other.

Wright Family Tree

CATHERINE
FREYER
1796–1889

JOHN
KOERNER
1791–1876

CATHERINE
REEDER
1800–1866

DAN
WRIGHT, JR.
1790–1861

SUSAN
KOERNER
WRIGHT
1831–1889

REUCHLIN
WRIGHT
1861–1920

LORIN
WRIGHT
1862–1939

WILBUR
WRIGHT
1867–1912

MILTON
WRIGHT
1828–1917

KATHARINE
WRIGHT
1874–1929

ORVILLE
WRIGHT
1871–1948

Two of a Kind

JUMP —IN THE— THINK TANK

Who or what would help you if you moved to a new town or school?

Mr. Wright traveled a lot for work. When he was away, he wrote hundreds of letters home. His letters helped the kids learn about places they'd never visited. During one of his trips he found the flying "bat" toy. Wilbur and Orville played with it until it broke. Their stores didn't have flying bats. What could they do?

The brothers got busy. They talked, planned, and built. They tested and failed. Then they tried again. Finally, they made a new bat. It flew!

Both Wilbur and Orville were hooked on flying.
They were alike in other ways, too. They were
funny and creative. They liked to build things
and play music. Wilbur played the harmonica,
while Orville played the mandolin. Both boys
were smart, too. Even their handwriting looked
the same! The brothers had their differences,
though. Wilbur was serious. He worked hard
at school and earned good grades. Orville joked
around. He often got in trouble at school. Orville
did his work, but he didn't always try hard.

> " From the time we were little
> children, my brother Orville and
> myself lived together, played
> together, worked together, and,
> in fact, thought together.
> —WILBUR WRIGHT "

Orville began building kites. He was just
10 years old, but they were good enough to sell

to his friends. Around this time, Wilbur started high school. He played sports like gymnastics and football. The family moved back to Dayton, Ohio. Wilbur was still a good student. He planned to go to Yale University after high school.

Then a hockey game changed Wilbur's life. A stick hit Wilbur in the face and knocked his teeth out! His whole face hurt. He even had to get false teeth. Wilbur was too badly injured to go to school. Then it got worse. He developed heart and stomach problems. Wilbur was sad. Instead of graduating high school and attending

Yale, he ended up staying home for three years.

At first, Mrs. Wright took care of Wilbur. Unfortunately, she needed help, too. She was sick with a lung disease called **tuberculosis**. Wilbur took care of her. He even carried her up and down the stairs.

Wilbur never went to Yale, but he didn't stop learning. Wilbur read books when his mom didn't need him. He read *a lot*. Orville had been busy, too. He wanted to have a business. Would Wilbur want to work with him?

The Wright family returns to Dayton, Ohio.

Wilbur gets injured during a hockey game.

WHEN?   **1884**   **1886**

CHAPTER 3

THE WRIGHT BUSINESSMEN

The Newspaper Business

When Orville was 12, he learned how a **printing press** worked. It was a machine that put ink on paper to make words and designs. A friend let him use a small printing press he had. Together they published a school newspaper. Orville later got a summer job in a print shop. Then Wilbur and Mr. Wright gave Orville his own printing press.

As Orville got older, he wished for a bigger, faster printing press. So he got to work. He used parts from an old buggy and a damaged **tombstone**. His self-inking press worked much faster, printing 500 sheets an hour.

Wilbur was finally feeling better, so the brothers went into the newspaper business together. They printed the first **edition** of *West Side News* on March 1, 1889. Sadly, not long after, their mother died of tuberculosis on July 4, 1889. The Wright brothers wrote about her death in their paper.

In 1891, Wilbur and Orville closed *West Side News* and printed more and more flyers and business cards for customers. The Wright brothers enjoyed the challenges of new experiences. It made sense—America was changing quickly in the 1890s. People didn't just use buggies and trains to travel anymore—they began to drive cars. And everyone wanted to ride a bicycle, including the Wright brothers.

The Wright Cycle Co.

How did Wilbur and Orville's childhood help them with their first business? How can your hobbies help you when you grow up?

The bicycle was the new **craze**. People left their horses at home and pedaled to work! They could even leave town with a friend. Some rode bicycles just for fun.

Orville was curious. He had to try it, so he bought a bicycle. Then Wilbur did, too. They pedaled near and far. The brothers soon figured out exactly how their bicycles worked. They started fixing bicycles for friends. In 1893, they were ready for a new business adventure. They opened the Wright Cycle Exchange. They became **mechanics**, fixing and selling bicycles.

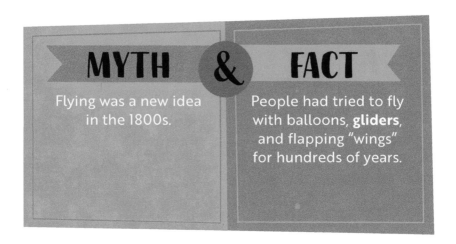

MYTH	&	FACT
Flying was a new idea in the 1800s.		People had tried to fly with balloons, **gliders**, and flapping "wings" for hundreds of years.

Business was booming. Wilbur and Orville changed the store's name to the Wright Cycle Company. They wanted to do more for customers. They knew how bicycles worked. So they started designing their own **models**. The Van Cleve bicycle was named for their

great-grandmother. It sold for $60 to $65 (almost $2,000 today). Their St. Clair model sold for just $42.50 (over $1,300 today).

Technology was moving fast during this time. The Wright brothers were excited for whatever would happen next. Could it be . . . a flying machine?

WHEN?

West Side News is published. Susan Wright dies.

The Wrights cancel the newspaper but keep the print shop.

1889   **1891**

The Wright Cycle Exchange opens.

The Wright Cycle Company sells its own bicycles.

1893   **1896**

CHAPTER 4

TAKING FLIGHT

Glide Like a Bird

When Orville was 25, he got sick after drinking unclean water. He caught a disease called **typhoid fever** and nearly died. Wilbur spent many worried hours beside his brother's bed in 1896. He used that time to read.

Wilbur read about a German man named Otto Lilienthal. Otto had built a glider, an aircraft designed to help a person fly. Gliders didn't need a motor. They used wind to fly. Otto made a lot of progress in human flight. He used his body to control his glider. Unfortunately, Otto's experiments ended when he died in a glider crash.

Wilbur wanted to know more about **aviation**. He read all the books and articles he could find. When Orville was awake, Wilbur read to him. Orville got better. He was curious about flying, too. The more they learned, the more excited they became about flying.

Wilbur and Orville talked a lot about flying. They did even more research. The brothers read about the work of **aviators** Octave Chanute and Louis Pierre Mouillard. What they learned thrilled them. Louis thought birds could teach people about flying. So Wilbur spent Sundays bird-watching.

JUMP
—IN THE—
THINK
TANK

What do you want to learn more about? What are some different ways you could learn about it?

Learning the secret of flight from a bird was a good deal like learning the secret of **magic** from a magician.

—ORVILLE WRIGHT

The brothers understood the four **forces** of flight:

1. **Weight** is the heaviness of an object.
2. **Lift** allows an airplane to come off the ground and stay in the air.

3. Thrust is the forward movement made by an aircraft's motor.

4. Drag is something that slows or stops an object from moving.

Weight is the opposite force from lift. Thrust and drag are opposites. When lift and thrust are strongest, the plane goes up. A plane flies level when the forces are equal. The brothers needed to find the right balance to keep an airplane in the air. Other aviators had tried for centuries. Could these two bicycle mechanics really find the answer?

Home Away from Home

Wilbur's bird-watching paid off. He noticed that when a bird raised the tip of one wing, it lowered the other wing. It reminded Wilbur of riding a bike. You move the handlebars to turn, but you also lean. Wilbur called it "wing warping" for flying. This was the discovery they needed! He had to show Orville how it worked. Wilbur squeezed the top and bottom of a cardboard box. One corner moved up. The other moved down.

It was the summer of 1899. Wilbur tested wing warping on a giant kite in a field. The kite proved that wing warping worked! Next, the brothers wanted to build a glider with the same controls as the kite. This new aircraft would carry a person. They talked, thought, and built. Then they needed wind to test the glider. Wilbur wrote a letter to the United States Weather Bureau. He asked them to suggest some windy locations. The small fishing village of Kitty Hawk, North Carolina, would be perfect. It had the wind they needed and lots of sand for soft landings. Wilbur and Orville traveled by train and then boat to Kitty Hawk.

They wanted to test the glider safely. Orville and their friend Bill Tate stayed on the ground. They held on to strings attached to the glider so that it wouldn't go too high. Wilbur lay flat in the middle, controlling the glider.

They spent six weeks flying the glider like a kite. Then it was time for the real test. They removed all the strings. Wilbur would glide on his own. On October 19, 1900, they achieved what they'd been working toward—Wilbur flew and controlled the glider!

After another visit to Kitty Hawk in 1901, the brothers returned to Dayton and got to work on a new way to test their gliders. They made a **wind tunnel**. It was a small box with air blowing through it. This device helped them test model gliders. It helped them understand how a full-size airplane might fly. After more testing, they returned to Kitty Hawk. Wilbur and Orville flew a new full-size glider in September and October 1902. They learned to control it. This glider flew over 600 feet! But the brothers weren't finished yet. Their glider worked, but they really wanted to create a flying machine. To do that, they knew one thing for sure: They needed a motor.

WHEN?

The Wright brothers control a kite with wing warping.	The Wright brothers test a glider in Kitty Hawk, North Carolina.	The Wright brothers successfully control a glider.
1899	**1900**	**1902**

CHAPTER 5
NEW HEIGHTS

It's a Plane!

Wilbur and Orville knew they'd made history in Kitty Hawk in 1902. They had controlled the glider in flight. No other **pilot** had ever done that. Next, they wanted to fly a powered airplane. No one had a motor that was both small enough and powerful enough. Wilbur and Orville would have to make their own. They didn't know enough about motors, but they knew who to ask for help.

Charlie Taylor already worked at the Wright Cycle Company as a mechanic. At the brothers' request, Charlie designed a motor. It was small *and* powerful.

Wilbur and Orville filled five notebooks with math and drawings for their new aircraft. They built it out of wood and called it the *Wright Flyer*. The motor made it heavy—around 600 pounds! To lift all that weight, the airplane needed bigger wings than their previous gliders. The *Flyer*'s wings were 40 feet, 4 inches wide. The brothers covered the wings with fabric like the earlier gliders.

Wilbur and Orville were the first aviators to add a **propeller** to an airplane. Propellers are like twisted wings that spin. Only boats had used them before. The *Flyer* had two wooden

JUMP
–IN THE–
THINK
TANK

The brothers kept track of the testing so they could see what worked best. How can you keep track of new things you try?

propellers, each eight feet long. With the propellers, wings, and motor, the *Flyer* would have enough lift and thrust to fly. The Wright brothers were ready to test the *Flyer*.

The First Flight

The brothers returned to Kitty Hawk, North Carolina, in September 1903. They made a 60-foot track so the *Wright Flyer* could have firm ground to gain speed. They called the track "Grand Junction Railroad."

Three months later, Wilbur and Orville were ready to fly. They tossed a coin to see who would pilot the *Flyer* first. Wilbur won. He got in and took off. The *Flyer* jerked up and down. It was in the air for 3.5 seconds . . . then the motor stopped and crashed into the sand. But the brothers were excited. They knew exactly what went wrong and how to fix it. They repaired the *Flyer* and waited for good weather. Three days later, they tried again.

The wind blew hard on the cold morning of December 17, 1903. It was Orville's turn to pilot the *Flyer*. The brothers shook hands. Orville lifted off the track at 10:35 a.m. For the *Flyer's* first real flight, he stayed in the air for 12 seconds. The flight was rough. Orville went up and down. But he flew for 120 feet!

WHERE?

OHIO

★ DAYTON

KITTY HAWK

NORTH CAROLINA

The Wright brothers took turns flying. The *Wright Flyer* flew four times that day. The longest flight was 50 seconds long.

The men were talking about flying again when a gust of wind blew. The wind slammed the airplane into the sand. The *Wright Flyer* never flew again.

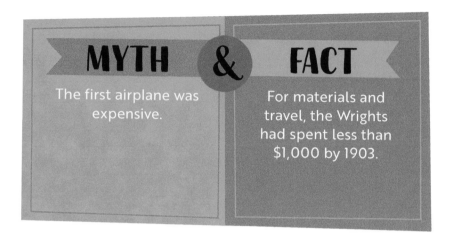

Still, Wilbur and Orville had to share the big news about their flights. Orville sent a **telegram** home. It began, "SUCCESS FOUR FLIGHTS THURSDAY MORNING..." Wilbur and Orville Wright's airplane **invention** would change their lives—and the world.

Wilbur and Orville fly the *Wright Flyer.*

1903 WHEN?

CHAPTER 6

FAME AND FORTUNE

Inventors and Businessmen

The 1903 flight in Kitty Hawk was important.
Wilbur and Orville didn't want someone else to
copy their work before they could sell it. So the
brothers applied for a **patent**. The patent would
make it against the law for anyone else to copy,
use, or sell an airplane like theirs.

They knew they could make airplanes more
useful. They wanted their airplanes to fly far and
long. Wilbur and Orville wrote a letter to the US
Army. The Army didn't want to buy their airplane without seeing it fly. They decided not to
fly for the Army—not yet.

In May 1904, the brothers began new tests
near Dayton. They used a cow pasture called
Huffman Prairie. Friends, family, and even
reporters gathered on May 26, 1904. The *Flyer II*
only got eight feet off the ground. Something
was wrong with the motor.

The brothers faced problems for the next three months, but they didn't give up. By August they were flying again. Wilbur flew in a complete circle on September 20, 1904. That flight lasted 1 minute, 36 seconds. The *Flyer II* flew 4,080 feet.

MYTH & FACT

The Wright brothers were instantly famous.

Newspapers and magazines weren't interested in reporting about Wilbur and Orville's flights.

Wilbur and Orville had a flying machine. The news began to spread. Some other flyers thought the brothers lied. That's because no one else was close to flying. The brothers knew they had to show the world. They were almost ready.

Trials and Travels

Wilbur and Orville made another airplane in 1905. The *Flyer III* had better steering and balance. Its motor was stronger. They flew it at Huffman Prairie. The Wright brothers were ready to sell their airplane. They finally got their patent in May 1906.

That year, French leaders wanted to meet Wilbur and Orville. Wilbur boarded a ship on May 18. Orville joined him two months later. They didn't fly. They attended meetings. They told people about their airplanes. They stayed until November.

Wilbur returned to France the next year. Orville packed one of their airplanes into crates and shipped it to Wilbur in France. But when Wilbur unpacked the crates in France, he had an awful time putting it back together. He discovered that many pieces were damaged or missing after the journey.

He finally finished rebuilding the aircraft. He had his first flight in France on August 8, 1908. The crowd cheered and shouted as he flew. He flew circles and figure eights. Wilbur became famous. The crowds grew to 200,000 people! He met royal families—kings, queens, princes, and more. Now the world believed the Wright brothers could really fly.

Around the same time, Orville was flying tests for the Army in Fort Myer, Virginia. Thousands of people watched. Everything went well until a propeller broke on September 17, 1908, and the airplane crashed. Orville's **passenger**

died, and Orville was badly injured. It took months for him to get better. When he could travel, he and his sister, Katharine, went to Europe to be with their brother. When they finally returned to Fort Myer, they flew more, showing that the airplane could travel 40 miles per hour with a pilot and passenger. Even though one of their planes had crashed, the Army was impressed. They bought an airplane.

The brothers weren't finished. Orville flew in Germany and France.

JUMP
—IN THE—
THINK TANK

Wilbur and Orville became famous, but they didn't change. Why do you think they stayed humble, kind, and hardworking?

WHERE?

BERLIN

FORT MYER

GERMANY

PARIS

FRANCE

A million people watched Wilbur fly over the New York Harbor. Everyone loved to watch the fliers.

WHEN?

Wilbur and Orville test the *Flyer II* at Huffman Prairie.

The *Flyer III* is a success.

Wilbur and Orville visit France.

1904 **1905** **1906**

Wilbur flies in Europe. Orville flies tests for the US Army.

Orville flies in France and Germany. Wilbur flies over New York.

1908 **1909**

CHAPTER 7

WEBBER & JOHNSTON
& SON .IT

BEYOND THE SKY

The Wright Company

Wilbur and Orville became known around the
world. People wanted to buy their airplanes.
So the brothers opened the Wright Company
in 1909. They built airplanes in Dayton, Ohio.
Wilbur was the president of the company, and
Orville was the vice president.

The Wright Company made more than a
dozen different kinds of airplanes. In 1910,
Orville flew the Wright Baby Grand model
80 miles an hour. They also started a flight
school that trained pilots to put on air shows.
Crowds gathered to watch pilots fly airplanes
and do stunts.

After the Wright brothers flew for the public,
other aviators copied their work. Wilbur and
Orville wanted to protect their patents. It upset
them to think of others selling airplanes with

their designs. In 1911, Wilbur went to Europe. This time he didn't fly for crowds. He was there for **court** cases. He explained why others should not use their designs. The judge in the court would decide who was right. There were many court cases in Europe and America. Wilbur and Orville won almost all of them. It was exhausting work. They missed experimenting and flying.

JUMP —IN THE— THINK TANK

Wilbur and Orville Wright invented an airplane because they worked hard and didn't give up. What dream do you have that you won't give up on?

In 1912, Wilbur got sick after eating bad oysters. Like Orville many years before, Wilbur had typhoid fever. His body was too tired. He couldn't fight it. Wilbur Wright died at home on May 30, 1912. He was 45 years old. Orville was devastated—he'd lost his best friend and business partner.

The Wright Legacy

Orville still needed to run the business. Now he had to do the work without Wilbur. Orville and the Wright Company continued to make new models of airplanes.

> **"** It is possible to fly without motors, but not without **knowledge and skill.**
>
> —WILBUR WRIGHT **"**

When World War I began, the government needed to know everything they could about flying. Patents no longer protected the Wright brothers' science and math. There would be no more court cases. But the business wasn't the same without Wilbur. Orville wanted to experiment again. He sold the Wright Company in 1915 and set up a **laboratory** in Dayton to test and research new inventions.

Orville was happy to get back to inventing. He made a racing airplane and other things, too. He designed a flying clown toy called "Flips and Flops." He also worked for the US government and the National Advisory Committee of Aeronautics (NACA), which would later become NASA. Today, they send rockets—and people— into outer space.

Orville saw his most famous invention do amazing things. In 1927, Charles Lindbergh became the first person to fly across the Atlantic Ocean by himself. Orville lived to be 76 years old. He died in Dayton on January 30, 1948, after a heart attack.

National parks have been created in North Carolina and Ohio to honor Wilbur and Orville Wright. Even France made a monument to celebrate the inventors. They received many awards and honors for being the first people to design and fly an airplane.

Neither Wilbur nor Orville Wright could have been the first to invent the airplane on his own. They needed each other. They thought as a team. They tested as a team. And they didn't give up,

even when flight looked impossible. These smart men persevered when things got tough—and they succeeded! That's why we honor and remember the Wright brothers today as the inventors of the airplane.

Wilbur and Orville create the Wright Company.

1909

Wilbur dies from typhoid fever at age 45.

1912

Orville sells the Wright Company and opens a laboratory.

1918

Charles Lindbergh flies across the Atlantic Ocean by himself.

1927

Orville dies after a heart attack at age 76.

1948

CHAPTER 8

SO ... WHO WERE THE
WRIGHT BROTHERS ?

Challenge Accepted!

Now that you know so much about the Wright brothers, let's see what you remember. This quiz will check your new knowledge of Wilbur and Orville Wright. Try to remember answers on your own, but you can also look back to find the answers to these who, what, when, where, why, and how questions.

1 Where did Wilbur and Orville live most of their lives?

→ A New York, New York

→ B Paris, France

→ C Washington, DC

→ D Dayton, Ohio

2 Who helped Wilbur and Orville learn the most when they were children?

→ A Their teacher, Mrs. Schoonover

→ B Their siblings, Reuchlin, Lorin, and Katharine

→ C Their parents, Milton and Susan

→ D Their librarian, Mr. Stackhouse

3 **Who in the Wright family was the first to get excited about flying?**

→ A Milton, the father
→ B Katharine, the sister
→ C Orville
→ D Wilbur

4 **How did Wilbur first discover wing warping?**

→ A Bird-watching
→ B Book reading
→ C Bicycle racing
→ D Kite flying

5 **Why did Charlie Taylor make a motor for the Wright Brothers?**

→ A The motor makers were too far from Dayton.
→ B The motor makers would take too long.
→ C The motor makers couldn't make a small, strong motor.
→ D The motor makers made motors too fast.

6 **Where did Wilbur and Orville fly the first airplane?**

→ A Dayton, Ohio
→ B Kitty Hawk, North Carolina
→ C Fort Myer, Virginia
→ D Paris, France

7 **How long was the first airplane flight?**

→ A 2 seconds
→ B 12 seconds
→ C 32 seconds
→ D 52 seconds

8 **When did the first airplane fly?**

→ A 1900
→ B 1902
→ C 1903
→ D 1905

9 **Why did Wilbur and Orville decide to fly in public?**

→ A To prove they had flown

→ B To fly figure eights

→ C To make their father proud

→ D To be on television

10 **What was the Wright brothers' most important accomplishment?**

→ A They started a newspaper called the *West Side News*.

→ B They built and sold bicycles.

→ C They learned a lot by reading.

→ D They built and flew the first manned airplane with a motor.

Our World

Our world changed because of Wilbur and Orville Wright. Let's look at what has happened after the Wright brothers' first 12-second flight.

→ Today, airplanes fly through the skies every day, bringing people closer together—and faster than other types of transportation. Flights travel between cities and continents. Today's airplanes can carry several hundred people at a time—or just a few. Every day, 2.7 million passengers fly in and out of the United States. As many as 5,000 aircraft are in the sky at the same time.

→ Airplanes carry more than just people. They move goods from place to place. Airplanes drop thousands of gallons of water on forest fires. Medical supplies and food can get to people in need quickly. The military also uses airplanes to protect the country.

→ Flights now go beyond our sky. In 1961, the first person flew in space. Neil Armstrong and Edwin "Buzz" Aldrin walked on the moon in 1969 while Michael Collins took pictures from space. Rockets blast into space today and visit other planets so we can better understand our solar system.

JUMP IN THE THINK TANK FOR MORE!

Now let's think about what Wilbur and Orville Wright did and how they changed the world we live in today.

→ How did Wilbur and Orville's work help inspire other aviators and inventors?

→ How does the perseverance of the Wright brothers make you want to work hard even when you face problems?

→ How do you benefit from Wilbur and Orville's invention of the airplane?

Glossary

American Civil War: The war in the United States between the Southern states and the Northern states from 1861 to 1865

aviation: Related to building and flying aircraft

aviator: A person who flies an aircraft

bishop: A person in charge of certain churches in an area

court: A place where decisions are made about people following the law

craze: A huge amount of excitement or interest in something

drag: The force of flight that slows or stops an object from moving

edition: A copy of a newspaper, book, or magazine

force: Something that causes motion or change

glider: A light aircraft made to fly without a motor

invention: A new discovery or creation

inventor: Someone who makes inventions

laboratory: A place to experiment with science

lift: The force of flight that allows an aircraft to stay in the air

mechanic: A person who fixes machines and motors

model: A design of something or a smaller version of something

passenger: Someone who travels in a vehicle but doesn't drive

patent: A legal document that protects an inventor's creation from being copied

pilot: A person who flies an aircraft

printing press: A machine that prints words and designs on paper

propeller: Spinning wings that move an aircraft

slavery: A system in which people are treated like property and forced to work against their will for no pay

telegram: A message sent by telegraph

thrust: The force of flight that produces forward movement made by an aircraft's motor

tombstone: A large piece of stone used to mark a grave

tuberculosis: A highly contagious and life-threatening lung disease

typhoid fever: A life-threatening disease caused by germs in food or water

weight: The heaviness of an object

wind tunnel: An enclosed or narrow area where wind is blown to experiment with air movement around an object

O

•

Bibliography

20th Century Time Machine. "Orville Wright, Wilbur Wright, Original Footage!!! First Flight Military Airplane, 1909." Last modified February 15, 2016. YouTu.be/dtZ8MxuePno.

Aviation History Online Museum. Accessed January 28, 2020. AviationHistory.com.

Britannica. "Wright Brothers: American Aviators." Accessed January 17, 2020. Britannica.com/biography/Wright-brothers.

CBS Sunday Morning. "The Story of the Wright Brothers." Last modified May 3, 2015. YouTu.be/Yjccw901Pwk.

Federal Aviation Administration. "Air Traffic by the Numbers." Accessed February 20, 2020. FAA.gov/air_traffic/by_the_numbers.

Freedman, Russell. *The Wright Brothers: How They Invented the Airplane.* New York: Holiday House, 1991.

Hazelgrove, William. *Wright Brothers, Wrong Story: How Wilbur Wright Solved the Problem of Manned Flight.* Amherst, NY: Prometheus Books, 2018.

Heppenheimer, T. A. *First Flight: The Wright Brothers and the Invention of the Airplane.* Hoboken, NJ: John Wiley & Sons, 2003.

Historic Wings. "The Wright's 'Other Achievements.'" Last modified December 17, 2012. Fly.HistoricWings.com/2012/12/the-wrights-other-achievements.

McCullough, David. *The Wright Brothers.* New York: Simon & Schuster, 2015.

NASA. "115 Years Ago: Wright Brothers Make History at Kitty Hawk." December 17, 2018. NASA.gov/feature/115-years-ago-wright-brothers-make-history-at-kitty-hawk

NASA. "The Four Forces of Flight." December 9, 2003. NASA
.gov/audience/foreducators/k-4/features/F_Four_Forces_of_Flight.html.

National Park Service. "Dayton Aviation Heritage National Historical Park,
Ohio." Accessed January 17, 2020. NPS.gov/daav/index.htm.

National Park Service. "Wright Brothers National Memorial, North
Carolina." Accessed January 17, 2020. NPS.gov/wrbr/index.htm.

Smithsonian National Air and Space Museum. "The Four Forces." Accessed
February 7, 2020. HowThingsFly.si.edu/forces-flight/four-forces.

Smithsonian National Air and Space Museum. "The Wright Brothers &
the Invention of the Aerial Age." Accessed January 17, 2020. AirAndSpace
.si.edu/exhibitions/wright-brothers/online.

Wilbur Wright Birthplace Museum. Accessed January 17, 2020.
WWBirthplace.com.

Woodford, Chris. "Propellers." Explain That Stuff! Last modified October 18,
2019. ExplainThatStuff.com/how-propellers-work.html.

Wright Brothers. Accessed January 17, 2020. Wright-Brothers.org.

About the Author

 **ANNETTE WHIPPLE** celebrates curiosity and inspires a sense of wonder in young readers while exciting them about science and history. She's the author of several books. Her recent titles are *The Laura Ingalls Wilder Companion: A Chapter-by-Chapter Guide* (Chicago Review Press) and *Whooo Knew: The Truth about Owls* (Reycraft Books). Annette is a former classroom teacher and still enjoys teaching children through her volunteer work with 4-H and her church. She also visits schools to share her passion for history, science, and words. When she's not reading or writing, you might find Annette snacking on warm chocolate chip cookies with her family in Pennsylvania. You can learn more about Annette's books and presentations at **AnnetteWhipple.com.**

About the Illustrator

ALESSANDRA SANTELLI was born in a small city near Milan in 1990. She still lives there with her family and her huge cat Michi. She grew up painting with tempera on the stones and making small illustrated books to sell to all her relatives. At that point it was fairly clear that she liked drawing, so she attended the Brera Fine Arts Academy in high school and the International Comics School. She currently collaborates with several Italian and foreign publishers and works in a studio that she opened with a colleague called Foglie al Vento. There, she likes to eat a lot of sweets while listening to David Bowie.

WHO WILL INSPIRE YOU NEXT?

EXPLORE A WORLD OF HEROES AND ROLE MODELS IN
***THE STORY OF*…** BIOGRAPHY SERIES FOR NEW READERS.

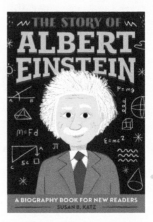

LOOK FOR THIS SERIES
WHEREVER BOOKS AND EBOOKS ARE SOLD

George Washington	Harriet Tubman
Abraham Lincoln	Barack Obama
Ruth Bader Ginsburg	Helen Keller
Frida Kahlo	Marie Curie

CPSIA information can be obtained
at www.ICGtesting.com
Printed in the USA
BVHW021755151121
621709BV00010B/48